MONTANA ON FIRE!
SUMMER OF 2000

Text by Michael Moore
Epilogue by Governor Marc Racicot
Published by Lee Montana Newspapers *and* Montana Magazine

Photography by Ken Blackbird, David Grubbs and Larry Mayer, BILLINGS GAZETTE
Jon Ebelt and George Lane, HELENA INDEPENDENT RECORD
Tom Bauer, Michael Gallacher, Tim Thompson and Kurt Wilson, MISSOULIAN
Derek Pruitt, THE MONTANA STANDARD
Lindsey Nelson and Joe Weston, RAVALLI REPUBLIC
Ashley Hyde and Craig M. Moore

KURT WILSON / *MISSOULIAN*

FRONT COVER:
Derek Pruitt/
The Montana Standard

BACK COVER:
(top) Tom Bauer/*Missoulian,*
(middle) George Lane/
Independent Record,
(bottom) George Lane/
Independent Record
(background photo)
Ashley Hyde

For more information on our
books, call or write:
Farcountry Press,
P.O. Box 5630, Helena, MT
59604, (406) 443-2842
or (800) 654-1105.

Book catalog appears online at
www.montanamagazine.com

Dedication

THEY CAME FROM THE OTHER SIDE OF THE
GLOBE AND FROM THE OTHER SIDE OF THE PASTURE.

NEIGHBORS HELPED NEIGHBORS. STRANGERS
HELPED STRANGERS.

BEFORE IT WAS OVER, SOME 12,000 FIREFIGHTERS
WERE AT WORK IN MONTANA, ONE OF THE GREAT-
EST PEACE-TIME MOBILIZATIONS IN THE HISTORY OF
OUR COUNTRY.

TO SOME, IT WAS ANOTHER ASSIGNMENT DURING
A LONG, GRUELING FIRE SEASON. FOR OTHERS, IT
WAS A FIGHT OF SURVIVAL, FOR THEIR LOVED ONES
AND THEIR PROPERTY.

THE FIRES WERE RELENTLESS. WHILE FIRE LOSS-
ES—MEASURED IN BURNED ACRES, HOMES, GRASS
AND TIMBER—WERE WIDELY REPORTED, FAR, FAR
MORE WAS SAVED. AND, MIRACULOUSLY, WITH NO
LOSS OF HUMAN LIFE AS OF THIS WRITING.

TO THE FIREFIGHTERS, FROM NEAR AND FROM
FAR, WE DEDICATE THIS BOOK.

1 VALLEY COMPLEX
176,000+ acres, 1,703 personnel

Burned southeast of Darby, both east and west of U.S. 93. The complex included a number of fires that burned together, for a total of more than 176,000 acres. When the Valley fires merged with the Mussigbrod complex, the new complex became the nation's largest of summer 2000. More than 1,700 firefighters and overhead personnel worked the fire, along with 80 engines, 12 bulldozers, 24 water tenders and nine helicopters. The Valley fires burned 66 homes.

2 MUSSIGBROD COMPLEX
84,939 acres, 469 personnel

The Mussigbrod fires burned 12 miles northwest of Wisdom, torching four structures and threatening the Springer Memorial community up the East Fork of the Bitterroot River after merging with the Valley fire. About 470 people were at work on the fire, with assistance from nine engines, four helicopters, five dozers and eight water tenders. Mussigbrod had burned nearly 85,000 acres by Sept. 2.

3 MAUDLOW-TOSTON COMPLEX
81,000 acres, 892 personnel

This fast-moving fire started northwest of Bozeman and scorched 81,000 acres before mop-up began in early September. Nearly 900 people were working on the fire by the time demobilization began. Because the fire threatened many homes, 46 engines and 34 helicopters were on hand here. They had help from eight choppers and 19 water trucks.

4 SKALKAHO COMPLEX
64,389 acres, 822 personnel

Burning north of the Valley Complex and just southeast of Hamilton, this group of fires burned more than 64,000 acres while threatening homes in the Sleeping Child and Skalkaho Road areas. These fires involved an intense structure-protection effort, using 46 engines and five helicopters, 19 bulldozers and 21 water tenders. Combined with the Valley fires, the Skalkaho complex helped fill the western Montana sky with smoke for a month.

5 WILDERNESS COMPLEX
63,307 acres, 38 personnel

The group of remote fires drew minimal attention from firefighters because it posed no direct danger to property. The fires did burn about 63,000 acres in the Selway-Bitterroot and Frank Church-River of No Return wilderness areas, about 15 miles southwest of Darby. Only 38 people, all part of an overhead team, worked the fire.

6 CANYON FERRY COMPLEX
43,947 acres, 1,221 personnel

This complex, made up of the Cave Gulch and Bucksnort fires on either side of Canyon Ferry Reservoir, was wrapped up and contained by September. It burned about 12 miles northeast of Helena, scorching more than 43,000 acres. The fires burned nine homes and forced hundreds from their houses in the last days of July. The Bucksnort fire was started by a man who'd thrown day-old charcoal briquettes away next to his driveway.

7 MONTURE/SPREAD RIDGE
27,500 acres, 191 personnel

These fires burned 27,500 acres about 10 miles north of Ovando before wet weather laid them low. About 191 fire personnel worked the blazes, with help from two choppers. Monture drew little attention because it posed little threat to homes and property.

8 STONE-YOUNG COMPLEX
25,330 acres, 482 personnel

This complex was made up of five fires—Lydia, Young, Stone Hill, Cliff Point and Fan Creek—and burned about 25,330 acres in the Kootenai National Forest southwest of Eureka. The fires were almost fully contained by Sept. 2 and some crews had been demobilized.

9 NINEMILE COMPLEX
24,350 acres, 1,223 personnel

Another five-fire complex, nearly 24,350 acres burned in the upper Ninemile Valley before torrential rains came on Sept. 1. More than an inch of rain fell in the Ninemile, the most received on any fire complex. The Ninemile fires drew significant attention, with 1,200 personnel on hand on Sept. 2. Nine helicopters helped out until rain and mud drove firefighters back to camp.

10 MIDDLE FORK COMPLEX
24,050 acres, 886 personnel

Thirty miles southwest of Philipsburg on the Beaverhead-Deerlodge National Forest, the Middle Fork Complex came to include eight fires: Middle Fork of Rock Creek, Falls Creek, Cougar Creek, Coyote Springs, Medicine Lake, Skalkaho Pass, Lick Creek and Cooper Creek. Cooler temperatures and less wind on the last of August, and some rain on Sept. 2, allowed containment.

11 CLEAR CREEK/RESERVATION
19,818 acres, 455 personnel

This group of three fires burned on the Flathead Reservation near Perma. More than 450 people were still working on the fires on Sept. 2, although two of the three blazes were almost fully contained. The fires burned just under 20,000 acres.

12 RYAN GULCH
17,118 acres, 649 personnel

This fire started near Interstate 90 and burned north of the highway between Bearmouth and Beavertail Hill. Just over 17,000 acres burned, 9,000 of which belong to Plum Creek Timber Co. Ryan Gulch forced evacuations and threatened power transmission lines. The fire also sparked concern about the ghost town of Garnet, but never got closer than five miles.

MONTANA ON FIRE!
Summer of 2000

Personnel totals show the highest number of people who worked on that fire at one time, and acreages are estimates as of September 2, 2000. Most fires saw little growth after early September, when rain moved across the state, dropping as much as an inch on some fires.

SASKATCHEWAN

NORTH DAKOTA

SOUTH DAKOTA

WYOMING

Havre · Malta · Glasgow · Wolf Point · Glendive · Lewistown · Harlowton · Roundup · MILES CITY · Big Timber · BILLINGS · Livingston · Red Lodge

Yellowstone National Park

N W E S

13 THOMPSON FLAT COMPLEX
14,936 acres, 678 personnel

A complex of six fires only three miles from Superior, these began the first week of August. After a fireline protected Superior, the fire blew up in mid-August and moved toward the small communities of Trout Creek and Quartz Flat, and moved on toward Sunrise and St. Regis. More and more firefighters were assigned to protect the settlements—and it worked; but some isolated cabins were lost.

14 KOOTENAI COMPLEX
13,711 acres, 434 personnel

This Kootenai National Forest fire group 20 miles northwest of Libby was contained by fireline on Sept. 1, the day after cooler and moister air moved in from the Pacific Northwest. Winds blowing down Lucky Point nourished the fire inside its lines even while mop-up continued.

15 BOULDER COMPLEX
12,604 acres, 909 personnel

Hundreds of homes were evacuated (but most of them saved), cattle herds turned loose or cut off from owners, and Interstate 15 and several state roads closed at times. Most of the losses were in pasturage and hayfields. Northwest of Boulder, the complex came to include the High Ore Road fire that threatened Elkhorn ghost town.

16 BLODGETT TRAILHEAD
11,486 acres, 257 personnel

The Blodgett fire forced the evacuation of the small community of Pinesdale, about three miles northwest of Hamilton. Although the fire had been working its way into the Selway-Bitterroot Wilderness in late August, more than 250 people still worked the blaze in early September, with help from two engines, two dozers and a pair of choppers. The Blodgett fire destroyed one home and numerous outbuildings while blackening about 11,500 acres.

17 BEAVER CREEK
10,800 acres, 607 personnel

Because it was south of the Big Sky resort area, this fire during the last two weeks of August had a high structural-protection priority. Rain and higher humidity finally helped firefighters halt its progress at month's end.

18 IDAHO FIRES
250,000+ acres, 250 personnel

Dozens of fires burned across a broad area of central Idaho. Total acreage burned exceeds 250,000 acres in the Salmon River drainage. More than half an inch of rain falling in areas of the Salmon–Challis National Forest has slowed the fires to a crawl.

ALL THE SIGNS WERE THERE BY MID-JULY.

Drought had become a constant, with thirty-five counties statewide classified as severe and another five, all in western Montana, on drought alert. Except in northeastern Montana, June, Montana's wettest month, had been almost absurdly dry. The state's forests were explosively parched.

Beyond the heated conditions lay a legacy of ninety years of fire suppression, a policy spawned in part by a cataclysmic series of fires that raged across the west in 1910. By waging war on fire, we had virtually ensured the inevitable—fires that even the most seasoned fire bosses could only gaze at in awe.

"The bottom line is, fire season is here," Ray Nelson, a spokesman at the Northern Rockies fire command, said on July 13.

Two days later, a ten-acre fire called the Little Blue blew up in the southern end of the Bitterroot Valley, running wild over more than 2,500 acres before day's end and forcing the first of thousands of evacuations.

Little Blue set the stage for the fiery play poised to unfold in the Bitterroot. During the next six weeks, more than 330,000 acres were scorched by intense fires set almost solely by a series of lightning storms.

Statewide, more than 840,000 acres had burned by early September and the end was yet to come.

"I'll tell you the truth about these fires," said Bobby Kitchens, a legendary Forest Service fire boss who worked as an information officer on the Valley Complex, the Bitterroot's most massive set of fires.

"There's almost nothing we can do about them. They're too big. We aren't going to put them out. The weather is the only thing that can put them out."

Kitchens' response—an atypical answer from the agency that pioneered wildland firefighting—was echoed time and time again by fire officials who agreed that the fires of 2000 were the worst since 1910.

While the Bitterroot burned brightest, it did not burn alone. Lightning-sparked fires raged between Helena and Bozeman, blackening the shores of Canyon Ferry Reservoir, torching houses in the almost-ghost town of Wickes, closing interstate highways and forcing thousands from their homes. The Maudlow-Toston fire, the state's second largest, burned more than 81,000 acres before the weather robbed it of its fearsome force.

The fires burned indiscriminately, on private and public land, through forest and over grassland, leveling the most primitive cabins and also scorching 7,000 acres of media magnate Ted Turner's Bar None Ranch near Maudlow. Thousands of Montanans were forced from their homes as fires threatened.

Seeking to limit new fire starts, Gov. Marc Racicot, the Bureau of Land Management and the Forest Service

GEORGE LANE/*INDEPENDENT RECORD*

CANYON FERRY COMPLEX *The community of York seemed like a ghost town after most of the residents had been evacuated in late July. About all that could be seen was one lone cat patroling the streets.*

closed access to more than 19 million acres of land in Montana. The closures meant that more than 20 percent of Montana's 94.1 million acres were off limits to the public, right at the height of tourist season.

"It's with great regret but with absolute conviction that I do this," Racicot said of the closures.

Although Racicot caused a furor by later claiming that the fires were partly a result of the Clinton administration's land-use policies, almost no one disagreed with the governor when he said the fire season of 2000 was Montana's worst disaster in the past half-century.

"We have not had a catastrophe of this magnitude in our lifetimes," the governor said on August 23.

Indeed, the nation endured its worst fire season in nearly a century. More than 6.3 million acres, most of it public, burned during the summer, and thousands of acres were still aflame in the Southwest and California as summer turned to autumn. Most startlingly, more than 42,000 acres burned in northern New Mexico when a prescribed fire in Bandelier National Monument got away in May. The Cerro Grande wildfire burned 245 structures in and around the town of Los Alamos and edged perilously close to the nation's largest nuclear weapons research lab. Ironically, most of the 1,000 acres the monument's managers meant to burn didn't.

Cerro Grande signaled the beginning of a fire season that simply defied firefighters. The hotshot team brought in to fight that fire thought they'd have it under control within a couple of days. Five days later they fled the fire as it crowned in fifty-mile-per-hour winds. By the time the fire was beaten back, the government had spent $32.5 million fighting it. That cost, however, was but a fraction of the expected $455 million compensation for Los Alamos residents who lost homes and property to the fire.

In size, the Cerro Grande fire paled next to the nation's largest fire of the year, the Hanford fire. That fire, started in late June by a fatal car crash, burned over 192,000 acres of rangeland, torching eleven homes and leaving one man with third-degree burns. The one bright spot: The fire moved across nuclear waste dumped on the Hanford Nuclear Reservation, but no radiation was released, according to the federal Department of Energy.

The bright spot in Montana came finally on September 1, when a cool front born in the Gulf of Alaska worked its way inland from the west coast. Combined with moisture moving north from the southwest, the storm brought a weekend's worth of rain to very thirsty country.

"This is going to be it," said Gene Rogers, a fire behavior analyst on the Valley complex. "This won't end it all, but it gets us headed in the right direction."

By September 5, Racicot and federal land managers reopened much of the state to the public, although burned areas remained closed and fires still shone across the state.

In early August, a fast-moving set of fires was burning in and along the western edge of the Selway-Bitterroot Wilderness. The wilderness becomes the Bitterroot National Forest as the country falls away into the valley below, and the forest then yields to private land. In firefighter parlance this intersection of wild country and development is known as the urban interface zone. It's a fancy phrase for trouble.

Ravalli County has been the state's fastest growing county, and many of those people have moved not into urban centers like Hamilton but up the gravel roads that snake back into the forested foothills of both the Bitterroots and the Sapphires, which border the valley's east side.

Many of the valley's new homes and subdivi-

BLODGETT TRAILHEAD *Flames and smoke rise above a home near Mill Creek in the Bitterroot Mountains close to Hamilton on August 1.*

sions have been built in low-lying ponderosa pine forests that historically burned every ten to twenty-five years. During the past century, as timber became valued and fire became feared, the Forest Service took fire out of the equation. Only fires burning in the deepest recesses of the wilderness were allowed to burn, and that step took place only in the past thirty years, as scientists realized the disastrous effect the lack of fire was having on the northwest's forests.

"Removing fire made these fires inevitable," said Jack Losensky, a retired Forest Service ecologist who specialized in the history of fire in the Bitterroot.

Before the 1870s, when white settlers moved into the valley, fire was a constant. Most blazes started with lightning strikes, but the Indian tribes that used the valley also set fires to keep their system of trails open. Those fires created a landscape that is nearly foreign to the valley today. On the valley floor and the lower foothills, park-like stands of ponderosas dominated. The big pines are genetically encoded to deal with fire, with thick bark that protects the tree from the low heat generated by the grass fires that swept through the valleys. Those fires routinely killed shrubs and encroaching Douglas-firs, a shade-tolerant species.

What was left was a sparse forest—maybe ten to twenty trees per acre—populated primarily by pines over 150 years old. When fires moved through such an area, they burned almost quietly compared to the raging infernos that lit the summer of 2000.

As fire disappeared, however, Doug-firs invaded the ponderosa lowlands, growing thickly under the shade of the towering pines. An acre that produced ten tons of

BOULDER COMPLEX Huge walls of flames leaped high into the night sky as they raced along this hillside near the town of Boulder. The fire was only a half mile away from Interstate 15.

fuel in 1900 produced more than thirty-five tons by 2000.

The firs and smaller pines also created a ladder that let fire crawl from the ground into the tops of even the tallest trees. Those fuel ladders helped create the wild torching fires that swept out of the Bitterroot's finger-like drainages in early August.

The valley's higher forests—the Doug and subalpine firs of the mid-slopes and the lodgepoles of the higher slopes—also became overgrown. Historically, those forests burned less frequently than the pine forests, but they still needed fire to clear the fuel loads created by dead and fallen timber.

NINEMILE COMPLEX *First Lt. Mara Campbell, Staff Sgt. Tracy Stringer, Sgt. Tim Allen and Brian Connelly of the Camp Pendleton, California Fire Department, from left, looked over maps of the Ninemile area where the soldiers would be deployed.*

"What has happened is that when fire comes, it's incrementally worse because there is so much fuel," Losensky said. "One of the biggest problems, and something we saw this year, is that the fire grows so quickly there isn't really time to get people in there to knock it down. By the time we're on it, it's too big and moving too fast."

In fact, one of the startling and more surprisingly aspects of the 2000 fires was the willingness of fire bosses to admit that, in many cases, there really wasn't much to be done.

"If we can get these fires to go in the direction we want, that's success," said Bobby Kitchens. "Right now, it's not really about trying to put them out."

For the most part, Montanans seemed to understand that fact, although there was a measure of grousing that firefighters moved too slowly to quell some fires.

"We understood that there was a risk of fire when we moved into this canyon," said Bayard Brattstrom, who lost his home in Laird Creek, a west-side drainage between Conner and Sula in the Bitterroot. "We knew that if a fire got down in here, there was a good chance that it couldn't be stopped."

The need to protect property and life at the expense of the landscape's health is a man-made conflict. Ecologically, the fires will have an overwhelmingly positive effect on the long-term health of Montana's forests.

"Even though we had very hot fires, they still will be very good for the environment," Losensky said. "The problem is that they burned in the interface, and that means we lost some property. If we were just dealing with fire, we would be okay. But we're dealing with houses and people's lives and that makes it very difficult."

When firefighters talked about their efforts in the summer of 2000, they almost always talked about public safety—their own included—and structure protection. One of the most cherished statistics on the Valley Complex was the one that almost never got talked about: How much property was saved, rather than how much was lost.

"So far, we've saved over $160 million in property from fire," said Alan Polk, an information officer on the Valley Complex. "That's why we're here."

Still, more than seventy homes burned in just the Bitterroot.

While media attention focused primarily on the threats to homes and property, Montana's wildlife endured the fires with little fanfare. While there were occasional reports of animals falling victim to flames, state wildlife managers were optimistic about the future. Working with information gleaned from the fires of 1988, particularly those in Yellowstone National Park, wildlife managers estimate that few of the state's large wildlife species suffered many losses.

"They tend to be able to sense the danger," John Firebaugh, regional wildlife manager for the state Department of Fish, Wildlife and Parks, told the *Missoulian*. "They seem to move away just far enough to get out of the fire's path. We have reports of deer carcasses found by firefighters. Some were in draws where I guess they thought they were safe. But those fast-moving fires just caught them. It's expected to lose a few individuals, but the overall population is not affected that much."

In fact, wildlife managers worried more in 2000 about the long-term affects of drought more than fire, which will likely improve conditions for wildlife over time.

"In the long run, most winter ranges will benefit from fire," Firebaugh said. "Fires recycle nutrients to get you more forage. It will open up some of the timbered valleys on the west side of the Bitterroot Valley…"

The morning of August 6 dawned warm and clear in the Bitterroot. The residents of Laird and Dickson creeks had been on formal evacuation notice for three days, but some had stayed with their homes, determined to protect them. Jury-rigged sprinkler systems were set up. Limbs got trimmed, trees close to homes felled. Julie Miller's Laird Creek home had a nice green space around it; she felt like it might survive a fire.

Bayard and Martha Brattstrom had done everything they could to fireproof their home, but they'd also loaded their valuables and important paperwork into their RV.

Far up Dickson Creek, Greg and Mary Tilford watched nervously as the Gilbert fire worked its way north. They knew their house probably couldn't be saved if wildfire rushed their ridge. Indeed, their local fire department had previously given them notice they wouldn't respond that far up Dickson Creek because the road was too narrow and rough.

The past week had been tense. A virtual ring of fire was closing ranks on the west side of the Bitterroots, marching north and east on the daily winds out of the southwest. Crews were working the fires, but most were in tough, almost inaccessible areas, where the battle was waged mostly by hand by understaffed crews. With fires raging all over the West, the Forest Service had already put almost every available firefighter to work. Private crews had trained and been hired. The military was pressed into action.

In an ordinary year, even an understaffed team might have stopped some of the fires that plagued the Bitterroot.

But not in the summer of 2000.

"We knew that if we got winds, we'd lose some houses," said Bobby Kitchens. "But what happened on August sixth, well, that was just a firestorm. No firefighters on earth could have stopped that. We're just lucky nobody got killed."

By mid-afternoon on that blue-sky Sunday, the winds began to pick up. The afternoon breezes had hampered firefighters for a week, whipping flames across freshly laid bulldozer lines. On the 6th, however, everything went to hell. The humidity dropped under twenty percent, a significant marker for fire activity. Winds that had topped out at twenty miles per hour in the morning doubled.

From a ridge east of Highway 93, Wannie Campbell videotaped the coming disaster, talking to herself as she taped. The Bear fire loomed behind her. Across the highway, a series of spot fires burning in Spade Creek began kicking up trouble. Worst of all, the Gilbert fire, recently combined with other, smaller fires, had literally exploded, forcing an awe-inspiring plume of smoke into the darkening sky.

Nearly everyone up Laird and Dickson creeks were in contact with their neighbors. In Dickson, they used hand-held radios, passing information back and forth as fire leapt from one ridge to another.

In Laird, the phone lines buzzed.

"At first we were checking the hillside every thirty minutes," Martha Brattstrom said. "By afternoon, we were looking every five minutes."

By 4:30 p.m., it was clear that Laird Creek would burn. Along with two other neighbors, the Brattstroms left the drainage, Bayard in the RV, Martha in the Subaru. They didn't even look back as the sky turned blood red.

"Sometimes you don't want to," Bayard said later.

By the time the Brattstroms reached the highway, the fire already was there. Blowing firebrands (flaming embers) over a half-mile, the storm leaped the East Fork of the Bitterroot River and the highway, then roared up the adjacent hillside. The Brattstroms met a team of firefighters on the highway, but the crew didn't even bother to pretend that the fire was something that could be fought.

"They just took pictures," Martha Brattstrom said. "They'd never seen anything like it."

Others taking pictures that day captured literal walls of flame dancing as high as 200 feet into the air. The description of the firestorm was almost always the same—the sound of an onrushing train barreling down the track.

"We heard the choo-choo train roar, and we felt the

heat," Martha Brattstrom recalled.

Just down the highway, Dickson Creek also went up in flames. Although natural fires threatened the drainage on both sides, some residents believe that the inferno that scorched their valley was started by fire-fighters.

They're called backfires or burnouts. The idea is to rob the main fire of fuel by burning in advance of its arrival. In an extraordinary fire season, backfires are a central weapon, in part because they can be lit far ahead of the main fire. That means that firefighters aren't put into danger-ous positions where they're staked along a fire front that can't be slowed down.

In situations where flames are approaching homes, backfires can be set to make sure the main fire doesn't run right up to houses. Backfires don't stop firebrands from setting fires, but they often stop ground fires and then slow crown fires blowing through the tree tops.

WILDERNESS COMPLEX *Some smaller tributaries of the upper Bitterroot River, including Laird Creek, will be affected immediately by the fires that burned along their drainage, but state fisheries biologists say the long-term effects tend to be beneficial for fish in general.*

"Backfires are one of the best tools we have," said Chris Papen, an information officer on the Bitterroot fires.

Forest Service officials have acknowledged that a fire was intentionally lit near homes along the East Fork between Dickson and Spade creeks. Wannie Campbell's videotape made it painfully clear that the backfire had unintended consequences, although it does-n't preclude the possibility that natural fire also blew into Dickson Creek on August 6.

"It's clear from the tape that the fire they started blew right up the mouth of Dickson Creek at a time when peo-ple were still in the drainage," Greg Tilford said later. "I'm sure that wasn't any-one's intent, but they had to real-ize that it was a possibility." A considerable amount of science is factored into backfires—relative humidity, wind speed and direction, time, distance to the main fire—but the backfire itself is more art than certainty.

"Obviously, working with fire poses a uncertain amount of danger, but it's a calculated risk," said Chris Papen. "But there is risk, and with the condition of these forests, that risk can't be discounted."

Despite the arguments over the genesis of the Dickson Creek fire, the aftermath produced only a profound respect for the power of fire. Up and down both drainages, homeowners sifted through the ashen remains of their houses. The fires had burned so hot that in most cases only stone and metal remained.

John and Alberta Snyder had built a cabin in Laird Creek in 1961, and they'd seen fire threaten the drainage more than once. John Snyder had come to believe that the canyon was somehow blessed, protected from fire by some unseen power.

Four days after the fire, Snyder poked through the remains of his home with a pitchfork.

"It used to be beautiful here," Snyder said through a sad smile. "The kids, the dogs, we all loved it."

Although Laird Creek looks as though it had been bombed, some homes in the drainage survived. Some made it for discernible reasons. Large grassy lawns kept the fire at bay, while metal roofs kept firebrands from igniting. But other homes, tucked into dense stands of trees, also survived.

"When the fire is blowing like this one, there's just no telling what might happen," said Pete Buist, a fire information officer from Alaska. "Sometimes, they just pick up like a tornado and miss one house altogether, then set back down and burn the next one."

BLODGETT TRAILHEAD *Wayne Stanford of the Three Mile Fire Department watched as the Blodgett Fire approached the Pinesdale area, four miles northwest of Hamilton.*

Some homes with lush lawns burned as well. Fire behavior analysts said that while a main fire may have skirted a house, a blowing ember might have landed on porch or even drifted through an open window.

"Sometimes you do everything right and you still lose it," Buist said. "Sometimes, nothing but divine intervention will do."

The same day that fire blew through the East Fork canyon and destroyed more than twenty homes, the Blodgett fire northwest of Hamilton roared out of Mill Creek and rolled over the southwest flank of the tiny community of Pinesdale. Residents there described a "ceiling of fire" sailing through the treetops. Rural fire departments from up and down the valley battled the fire, and, incredibly, only one home on Pinesdale's fringe was incinerated.

More than one resident of Pinesdale, a community bound by its religious beliefs, proclaimed that the hand of God had saved the town.

More often than not, it was firefighters, working hand in hand with meteorologists, fire behavior analysts and seasoned commanders that protected property. Even in situations where some homes were lost, what was remarkable was that the losses weren't more extensive.

"Given the number of homes in the interface, it's really sort of amazing that we didn't lose more houses, particularly on the sixth," said Ellen Bonnin-Bilbrey, who worked on the Bitterroot fires.

Because the fires burned so intensely and were often fanned by heavy winds, planning was critical as fire bosses made their daily calls on where to position firefighters. The plans often had their start with men like Chris Gibson, a meteorologist from Salt Lake City, and Gene Rogers, a fire behavior analyst from Klamath Falls, Oregon.

Fire works along three fault lines: fuel, topography and weather. Although fuel loads and topography change as the fire moves through different country, they are at least quantifiable and understandable variants in a very complex equation. The weather is the wild card.

"People often talk about fires creating their own weather, and to an extent they do," said Gibson, a National Weather Service employee who pulls fire duty every summer. "But ninety-nine-point-nine percent of the time, the weather controls the fire. The weather is the reason the fire does what it does."

In the Bitterroot, Gibson provided a forecast far more precise and varied than the kind provided to the general public. Hooked by satellite to nearly every weather source available, Gibson predicted winds—both speed

A bicyclist wearing a respirator signals for a turn in downtown Missoula on August 3.

and direction—temperature and relative humidity at a variety of altitudes. With heavy smoke hanging in the valley, Gibson also predicted inversions, which were a mixed blessing throughout the summer.

Although smoke choked the Bitterroot from Sula to Missoula, the hazy pall kept temperatures down, particularly during a hot stretch in mid-August where the mercury soared over ninety degrees any time the inversion cleared. Those cooler temperatures helped firefighters at a time when the fires were all but unapproachable.

The cooler temperatures weren't much relief to the general public, which spent most of the summer under one sort of air advisory or another. In Missoula, health officials repeatedly called Stage 2 air alerts, a scenario usually played out in winter. And the air was noticeably worse in the Hamilton area.

Smoke posed yet another consideration for meteorologists and behavior analysts—could planes and helicop-

CANYON FERRY COMPLEX *Retardent is dumped on the west slope of the Spokane Hills, on the west side of Canyon Ferry reservoir.*

ters work the fire from the air? Obviously retardant drops from air tankers and water drops from choppers were key tools in the firefighters' arsenal, but flight also let fire bosses see what was happening in a way that reconnaissance from the ground never could.

Gene Rogers used both visual observation and infrared pictures to make decisions about where firefighters could do the most good, but, more importantly, do so safely.

"My job is all about safety," said Rogers, who became a behavior analyst only after eighteen seasons of firefighting experience. "When analysts make mistakes, the truth is you learn about them through injuries or deaths. I don't want to be responsible for someone dying on the line."

Rogers' job is to bring some level of certainty to a world of what-ifs. If the fire is burning downslope on a south-facing ridge in heavy timber, how fast will it move? What time of day will be most dangerous? What are firefighters' best escape routes given the lay of the land?

"It's an inherently dangerous job, but we've got to give those guys the best information so that we don't have a tragedy," Rogers said.

In part owing to experts like Rogers and Gibson, Montana did not lose a firefighter during the extraordinary fire season. Nationwide, at least nine fighters died in fires scattered from California to Mississippi.

Although firefighters used their historical tools—

pulaskis, shovels and water—to battle the 2000 blazes, firefighting has changed since July 1994, when fourteen firefighters died in the South Canyon Fire on Colorado's Storm King Mountain. Fearful of losing their crews to the incredibly hot blazes, fire bosses often kept firefighters off the fires' advancing lines. Instead, they used retardant drops from huge air tankers that flew out of Missoula and Helena all summer long, coupled with water ferried by helicopters.

When they did work in front of the fires, they did so far ahead of them. Using bulldozers and hand tools, fire crews cut miles and miles of containment lines, then burned back toward the big fires in hopes of cutting down fuel loads that fed the blazes.

"We're willing to put people in the field, but we're not willing to get them killed," said Gene Rogers. "We've learned those lessons."

That practice occasionally drew jeers from home and property owners who lost grass, timber and buildings to the fires, but no one died.

"There's not one house out there worth somebody's life," Rogers said.

A life, perhaps, is a thing that can't be valued. But nearly everything else about a fire can be. The wildfires of 2000 came at massive expense to state, local and federal governments. Nationwide, more than $18 million per day was spent fighting fires. Estimates showed the country would likely spend more than $1 billion battling the summer's conflagrations.

By the first of September, about $142 million had been spent in Montana alone. While some crews were being sent home less than a week later, that cost was expected to climb until the snow flew. In fact, state budget officials said it could take years before the final costs are figured out.

Nothing about firefighting is cheap. A crew of twenty experienced firefighters costs $2,500 per day. But more than that is spent on one drop from a P-3 retardant tanker. The big planes dump 3,000 gallons of retardant per run, and the retardant alone costs $2 per gallon. The plane itself costs about $2,800 per hour to fly. Assign a couple of heavy lift helicopters to a fire and you can spend another $60,000 in a day.

At one time during the summer, more than 12,000 firefighters were at work in Montana, men and women from 26 states and Puerto Rico, plus New Zealand, Australia, and Canada.

On average, the Forest Service figures it costs over

NINEMILE COMPLEX *Gary SkunkCap loaded Gatorade for distribution at the Ninemile area fire camp, which he said used as many as 500 cases of that drink and bottled water in a day.*

$1,000 per acre to fight a fire. Of course, the costs vary widely depending on what sort of effort goes into the fire. For instance, the government had spent about $520,000 on the Wilderness Complex fires of the Bitterroot by late August. Those fires had scorched about 60,000 acres.

Burning not far from the Wilderness Complex was the Valley Complex, which contained the nation's largest

BITTERROOT COMPLEX *A burned land-sale sign leans against the scorched trees on a parcel of land in the Bitterroot Valley.*

fire. The Valley was also one of the country's more expensive fires, primarily because it threatened more than 1,000 homes and destroyed more than 65. Valley Complex fires burned about 170,000 acres, but the government spent more than $15 million battling them with more than 1,000 firefighters at a time.

Obviously, the costs didn't end with the firefighting efforts. Although it was too early to even guess at rehabilitation costs by late summer, President Clinton already had asked for $1.2 billion for rehab and forest management. At Gov. Racicot's request, Clinton also declared the state a disaster area, making it eligible for relief money.

FEMA also was in the state looking to help both residents and businesses right themselves after the fire. FEMA had money available to compensate losses not just of property, but of lost business.

Statewide, more than 6,000 people were out of work because of the fires, and estimates of business losses ran to as high as $3 million per day.

Some of that loss came in the wood products industry, which essentially shut down in western Montana over the summer of 2000. But once the smoke clears, salvage logging operations begin. Just a month after 15,000 of 23,000 acres burned in the Sula State Forest in early

August, for example, three salvage operations were in progress there. As much as 25 million board feet of timber may be salvaged out of the Sula forest, and it is but a sliver of what burned in the West during 2000.

Meanwhile, the traditional forces aligned themselves in the debate over what ought to be done with all that scorched timber. Loggers were ready to cut it and get it to mills, while environmental groups wanted timber managers to go slowly and evaluate the value of the blackened trees to the ecosystem.

In an interview with the *Missoulian*, Dale Bosworth, the regional forester for Montana and north Idaho, said the agency won't solely be in the timber business.

"This time, I'm suggesting that a byproduct of getting the land into the condition we want, might be some forest products," Bosworth said. "Our approach will be completely different. The focus won't be on how many million board feet we can salvage, but on how many acres we need to rehabilitate."

Bosworth's sentiment was considerably different than that of forest managers after the last round of major wildfires. "At this stage in the 1988 fire season, the chain saws were already running," Bosworth said. "Fire was much more evil and a little less understood."

On private land, timber companies went to work quickly with landowners to make plans for salvage.

GEORGE LANE/*INDEPENDENT RECORD*

CANYON FERRY COMPLEX *A helicopter pilot filled his bucket from Canyon Ferry Reservoir and prepared to make the short flight back to the fire.*

Stimson Lumber had fielded more than 100 calls by early September from landowners anxious to do something with their burned timber.

Timber companies also had to deal with the effects of fire on their own lands. Plum Creek Timber Company had 16,000 acres of land affected by ten fires. Most of the land was east of Missoula, where the Ryan Gulch fire burned more than 17,000 acres between Beavertail Hill and Bearmouth along Interstate 90. More than half that acreage belonged to Plum Creek, including a stand of trees that had been thinned specifically to fend off fire and disease.

Although the majority of fires that burned across both the west and Montana started with lightning strikes, some of the state's most destructive blazes were caused by people.

The Ryan Gulch fire, for instance, was ignited by a man running a chain saw.

Near Red Lodge a speeding motorcyclist lost control while roaring up the Beartooth Highway. As the cycle careened through some rocks, sparks set a fire that grew quickly to 3,000 acres, prompting the evacuation of 150 homes and closure of the famous scenic highway.

And on July 22, a man living on Elkhorn Road near Canyon Ferry Reservoir east of Helena had a barbecue. The next afternoon, the man cleaned up the grill and tossed the used charcoal briquettes alongside his driveway. Later in the afternoon, winds blew embers from the still-smoldering charcoal into a dry, grassy gully next to the driveway. The fire burned for a while undetected, and was a fully formed wildfire by the time firefighters were called in.

As that fire, dubbed the Bucksnort, roared to life, a second fire called Cave Gulch started on the west side of the reservoir above Kim's Marina. Fighting the fires became secondary as volunteers, firefighters and law officers scrambled to evacuate the heavily populated shores of the reservoir.

In the world of firefighting, some teams are set up to do initial attacks. Volunteer crews arrived quickly on the Bucksnort fire, but it mushroomed through the Spokane Hills so fast that the notion of knocking the fire down became ludicrous.

"We went into structure protection mode," Ken Mergenthaler, chief of the Eastgate Volunteer Fire Department, told the Helena *Independent Record*.

About that time, Cave Gulch took off. Staffing the fires soon became a high-wire act, with fire bosses shuttling crews to areas where homes and lives were most likely threatened. On that first day, that meant keeping crews on the Bucksnort fire, which imperiled far more homes than Cave Gulch. Before the day was out, every firefighter in the Helena Ranger District was at work, and crews from Lincoln and Townsend moved closer to Helena to deal with any new fires.

"Moving pieces around the board," said Dave Turner, an information officer for the Helena National Forest.

GEORGE LANE/*INDEPENDENT RECORD*

CANYON FERRY COMPLEX *The Spokane Hills are alive with color as a result of the Bucksnort Fire. A lone firetruck sat and watched for any flareups.*

"It's like a chess game."

What happened in the Cave Gulch-Bucksnort fires was mirrored around the country. Bucksnort got most of the attention because it threatened houses. In a year when resources were stretched perilously thin around the nation, Cave Gulch got less attention than it might have. As a result, the fire lingered between 1,000 to 2,000 acres at a time when it might have been extinguished or at least contained. Then it exploded. By the

Toston. The Boulder Complex, made up of the Boulder and High Ore fires, ultimately burned more than 12,500 acres just northwest of Boulder. They came to life in early August, forcing evacuations and highway closures. The High Ore fire alone forced people out of nearly 500 homes in the Basin-Boulder area, and led to a temporary closure of Interstate 15 between Boulder and Butte.

After being slowed down by weekend rain, the Boulder Complex fire was brought back to life by dry winds on

ASHLEY HYDE

MAUDLOW-TOSTON COMPLEX *Fireball near Deep Creek.*

end of August, Cave Gulch had blackened more than 29,000 acres. Some of that acreage contained valuable, old-growth trees that in another, more routine fire season might have drawn attention and firefighters.

But timber was an afterthought during the fires of 2000. Nearly the entire firefighting effort that fanned out across Montana was devoted to safeguarding property.

"In an ideal world, we would have sufficient resources and we would have zoning to keep homes out of areas out of high fire risk," Tom Clifford, supervisor of the Helena National Forest, told the *Independent Record*. "If that was the case, then the Forest Service could return to fighting forest fires instead of concerning itself with protecting structure. Until then, this is something society is going to have to deal with."

Structure protection was key in fires that raged near Boulder and the small farm towns of Maudlow and

August 7. One fire crew, Blackfeet 1, was chased onto a rocky "safe zone" they had scouted near the High Ore fire. Squad boss Consaida Birds told the *Independent Record*'s Carolynn Farley that her crew had to wait for two hours until the fire cooled enough for them to return to the line.

On that same day, the High Ore escaped fire lines and burned right through Boulder Valley rancher Dave Reider's herd. "You just swallow it and take it and hope the losses aren't too bad," he told Farley. "We're so ignorant of a fire of this magnitude. You don't really know what could happen." But, for his cows, "If they can get out of the fence, we figure they've got a chance."

In late August, a blustery afternoon wind pushed the Maudlow-Toston out of control once again, forcing officials to close thirty-three miles of Highway 12 east of Townsend. The blaze that kept fire fighters, residents and livestock on the run had its mid-August beginning in a grain field. In one afternoon, the fire burned over seven miles in six hours. It also caused a major power transmission line that ferries electricity from Colstrip to the West Coast to shut down briefly as the fire burned beneath the towers.

On August 23, Peggy Flynn of the historic Hidden Hollow Ranch east of Townsend, complained to Martin J. Kidston of the *Independent Record* that the Maudlow-Toston fire perimeter was too large. "This is mostly private pasture and timber burning up," she said. "It gets real frustrating when your livelihood is burning up."

But the extreme winds made fire officials look to firefighter safety as well, even while expressing sympathy for ranchers. Bill Branham, Planning Section Chief on the fire, said that weather, resources, cost and terrrain also had to be considered. Working closer to the fire was an option—then dismissed because it was too dangerous for fire crews.

Anticipating fall feeding, though, Peggy Thompson, with husband Jim a partner in a Dry Creek cattle operation, said, "We're just waiting to see if we have any pasture left. Our only option otherwise will be to take the cattle to North Dakota."

Ranchers looking for their runaway cows also noticed significant fish kills in the Dry Creek area between Maudlow and Toston. State wildlife officials and ranchers also worried that valuable winter range—for both cattle and big game—went up in flames, creating the possibility of competition once snow fell.

The current legacy of fighting wildland fires sits squarely at the feet of the fire season of 1910.

"August of 1910 was the single most important moment in American fire," fire historian Stephen Pyne said during a July visit to Montana. "It burned a swath across the memory of a generation of foresters."

During the second week of August 1910, the Forest Service was a fledgling agency still finding its footing, still trying to understand the role of fire in America's forests.

Three years earlier, foresters had declared that, given enough men and resources, they could protect the woods from fire. But the foresters had never envisioned anything like the storm that blew into the inland northwest on August 20, 1910.

On that day, hundreds of fires were burning in Montana and north Idaho. The country had literally been lit up by a series of lightning storms in June and July; by August, a national call for help had gone out.

On the twentieth, a dry cold front blew into the Bitterroot, kicking hurricane force winds ahead of it.

"Hundreds of fires merged into one maniacal blaze that marched up the mountainous backbone separating Montana from Idaho," *Missoulian* reporter Sherry Devlin wrote about the 1910 fires. "Towns and homesteads burned as frantic citizens buried their belongings and boarded rescue trains. Firefighters had time only to cover their heads with blankets and take refuge in creeks and mine shafts; seventy-eight of them died during the firestorm's passing."

"All resistance crumpled," Pyne told the *Missoulian*. "Crews fled from the hills, camps disintegrated into ash, pack trains vanished."

What ultimately vanished was the notion that fire had any place in the forests. Gifford Pinchot, the former chief of the Forest Service, glorified the efforts of the firefighters, suggesting that with enough men, a better trail system and more money, the fires of 1910 could have been stopped.

"So the argument then became that the only way to stop these fires—to prevent them from happening again—was to develop the country as rapidly as possible," Pyne said. "Build roads into the forests. Build trails. Until we did that, we were not going to be control these wildfires."

Henry Graves, who'd become chief after Pinchot and presided over the Forest Service when the fires struck, declared the agency's new resolve: "The necessity of preventing losses from forest fires requires no discussion. It is the fundamental obligation of the Forest Service and

IDAHO *Fifty-seven firefighters killed in the 1910 fire are buried in the Woodlawn Cemetery in St. Maries, Idaho. Among the headstones are eight marked simply "Unknown." Firefighters had been gathered so quickly that crew bosses did not know all their names.*

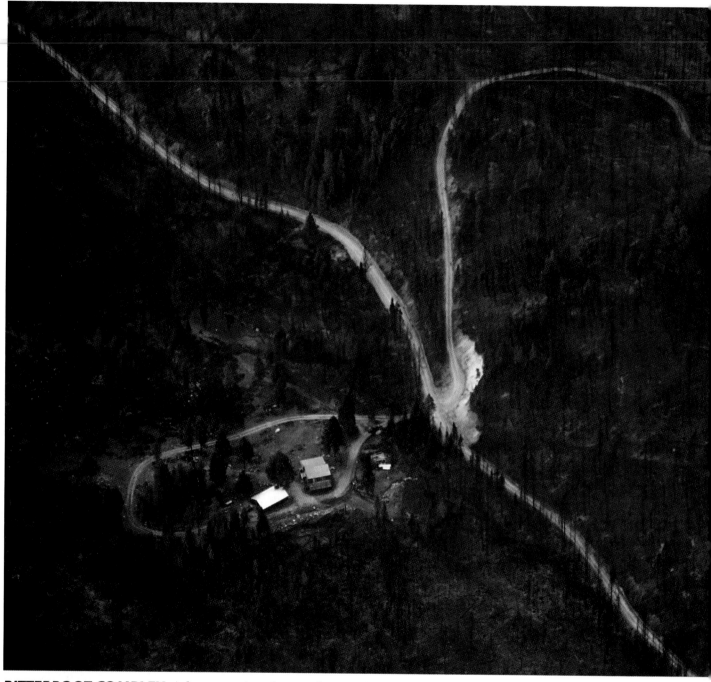

BITTERROOT COMPLEX *A home survives despite the scorched landscape surrounding it in the Bitterroot Mountains south of Darby.*

takes precedence over all other duties and activities."

In place of concern over the forest's overall health, the agency turned its focus to making the forests safe for people.

Said Steve Arno, a fire ecologist who recently retired from the Forest Service's Intermountain Fire Sciences Laboratory in Missoula: "The idea wasn't 'Well, we're going to adapt our communities and we're going to adapt our forest management to the inevitability of fire.' That wasn't the viewpoint. It was, 'We are going to make the forest environment safe for people. We are going to do our best to eliminate fire from the forest. Because fire

isn't needed, we will be better off if we just do our best to get rid of it'."

Of course, fire couldn't be entirely eliminated from the country's forests. But the Forest Service did succeed most of the time, knocking out ninety-eight percent of fire starts. For instance, in 1939, about 1.3 million acres burned in the West. In 1952, less than 300,000 acres burned.

Slowly, the farsighted within the Forest Service began to realize that fire's absence was causing problems in the woods. It seemed almost silly to fight fires that posed no threats to homes and might help regenerate the forests.

As early as 1972, fire began its comeback. Interestingly enough, that return started in earnest in the Selway-Bitterroot Wilderness. During that first experimental fire season, only one fire started in the study area—it burned about 500 square feet. The next year gave foresters a better look at what might happen as fire returned to the ecosystem. About 2,800 acres burned in the wilderness that summer.

The agency's wilderness fire program grew incrementally through the next fifteen years, until 1988, when a fire in the south end of the Scapegoat Wilderness blew out of control and raced onto the Rocky Mountain Front. That fire, known as Canyon Creek, burned over thirty miles in sixteen hours.

"Nobody alive had ever seen that kind of fire behavior," said Orville Daniels, who was then supervisor of the Lolo National Forest and who gave the original order to let Canyon Creek burn. "It was the fastest rate of spread ever recorded in North America. Canyon Creek taught us what was possible."

Although the fire, along with those in Yellowstone National Park the same year, helped bring a temporary halt to the national fire program, it did not disappear. The Forest Service and other federal agencies have continued to use fire—often prescribed fires set in controlled circumstances—to help revive unhealthy forests and rob them of excessive fuel loads.

The inherent problem, about which there is little disagreement, is that the northwest's forests have become so thick with timber that simply returning fire to the woods is too dangerous.

"We shouldn't try to put natural fire back under these very unnatural conditions of super-dense stands where fire has been kept out for way too long," said Steve Arno. "We need to reduce the fuels first and save the big trees that should be there and get it so we can safely put fire back in. We've got to preach an entirely new message."

How Montana and the rest of the west hammer out that message is yet to be decided. Old and persistent divisions are active, between the logging community and some environmental groups, between conservation and resource development, between wilderness lovers and those who'd rather see roads accessing the last vestiges of Montana's unbroken forests.

With the fires still raging, Montana Governor Marc Racicot and other Republicans began blaming the Clinton-Gore administration for the fires. Racicot later tempered his criticisms and pledged to work with the Forest Service to help restore balance to the western woods, but other Republicans piled on, trying to turn the fires into election-year fodder.

Said a spokeswoman for Idaho Rep. Helen Chenoweth-Hage when President Clinton visited Idaho during the fire season: "President Clinton came to Idaho to watch Idaho burn and tell us he felt our pain. Clinton felt our pain because he caused it."

Editorial pages in the state's newspapers came alive with debate over roadless policy, logging and fire. Too often, the public arguments were simplistic. Logging forces placed too much faith in the ability of their craft to recreate healthy forests, while environmental groups were too quick to see loggers as simply wanting to make a quick buck off the fear of future fires.

The debate waged nationally as well, often in hyperbolic terms.

"Nature sometimes has suicidal impulses," Lance Morrow wrote in the September 11 issue of *Time* magazine. "This year in the American West, it has set itself on fire—fire's version of The Perfect Storm, a convergence of dry summer lightning, blast-furnace air and millions of acres of tinder. The worst is yet to come."

The problem, of course, is far grander than any editorial-page or magazine debate is going to solve. Forest managers estimate that there are about 40 million acres of ponderosa pine forests that need both thinning and burning. And it's not a matter of thinning and burning once. Ponderosa forests previously burned as regularly as every ten years and still need to.

Orville Daniels once estimated what the Lolo National Forest would have to burn to create forests that

BOULDER COMPLEX *The Ontario 13 Crew heads to a flare-up on the High Ore side of the Boulder Complex fire. The Boulder Valley, in the background, is filled with smoke.* CRAIG M. MOORE

looked and functioned the way nature intended them to.

"On the Lolo, I figured we would have to burn 300,000 acres a year in the ponderosa-pine types to keep those stands in a condition that would mimic nature," Daniels told the *Missoulian*. "And that was only one forest type. I'd still have another million acres that needed something else."

Daniels and others who realized the need for fire early on were visionaries, but implementing that vision won't be easy. It may not even be possible. It may simply be that for all man's planning, fire will have its say.

The world was once ruled by nature, by fire, earthquake, flood, hurricane. Early man adapted, living where nature allowed, where her patterns gave him the advantage. Foods such as mushrooms were plentiful after fire. Fire kept man's travel routes open. Fire, whatever its disadvantages, gave life.

But as humans settled, they found less and less need for fire. Eventually it became an evil to be stamped out. For decades in modern America, that message was prevalent. "Only you can prevent forest fires," Smokey the Bear told us.

But fire will not be denied.

"Fire is not going away," said Bobby Kitchens, who has seen more than his share. "This is a big country, with a lot of forests. Fire is going to happen, whether we put it there or whether it comes out of the sky. There's just no getting around it. To come to terms with fire, we've got to see it in a different light."

Kitchens and the thousands of firefighters who called Montana home for a brief time this summer are part of a mythological breed, something akin to the cowboy. The story of firefighting is heroic and brave, a titanic battle fought against an epic foe.

"There is this grand story of firefighting," Pyne told the *Missoulian*. "There was this immense and heroic fire, and an immense and heroic response."

But fire has its own story. For eons, it was written on a landscape formed precisely by and for the telling. It was central to the larger story of how the earth renewed itself. Perhaps that chapter is over. Maybe fire can be managed beneficially. But it will not be easy.

This summer and for every summer in the foreseeable future, the woods are thick with trees. The summers of the West are arid and hot. Lightning is one storm front away. Fire will come again.

BUTTE *An early-morning sun, reflected in a small pond on the Continental Divide near Butte, appears orange through smoke from area forest fires*

SKALKAHO COMPLEX
The Bear fire burns in the Bitterroot Mountains southeast of Darby.

BLODGETT TRAILHEAD *Levi Brubaker waters down the roof of his uncle's house near Pinesdale, with the Blodgett fire approaching.*

NINEMILE COMPLEX *Jason Werner, a mechanic, inspects a helicopter's water-dumping bucket.*

MUSSIGBROD COMPLEX *Starving and burned on all four paws, this black bear cub was rescued near the East Fork of the Bitterroot, and sent to a wildlife refuge in Helena to be healed before being returned to the wild.*

BITTERROOT COMPLEX *Two elk take refuge in the East Fork of the Bitterroot River as flames consume a hillside.*

Facing page: **ALDER CREEK FIRE** *A Sikorsky Sky Crane flies over the Alder Creek fire in the Rock Creek drainage, a lightning-caused blaze. Water is dumped from the black tank; the hose is for refills.*

KOOTENAI COMPLEX *Bill Smith of Eureka walks to son Bruce's cabin in the shadow of a fire ten miles southwest of Eureka, ready to help move out belongings.*

SKALKAHO COMPLEX *East of Darby, the planning tent was but one tent in a city of them set up by the Forest Service for fighting the Valley Complex fires.*

NINEMILE COMPLEX *U.S. Army soldiers from Fort Hood, Texas, unload duffel bags upon their arrival at the Ninemile Fire Camp.*

MICHAEL GALLACHER/*MISSOULIAN*

THOMPSON FLAT COMPLEX *A member of the Del Rosa Hotshot crew from San Bernardino, California, hoses down hot spots on the Land-owner Mountain fire west of Superior. His crew was setting burnout fires to save a house in the fire's center.*

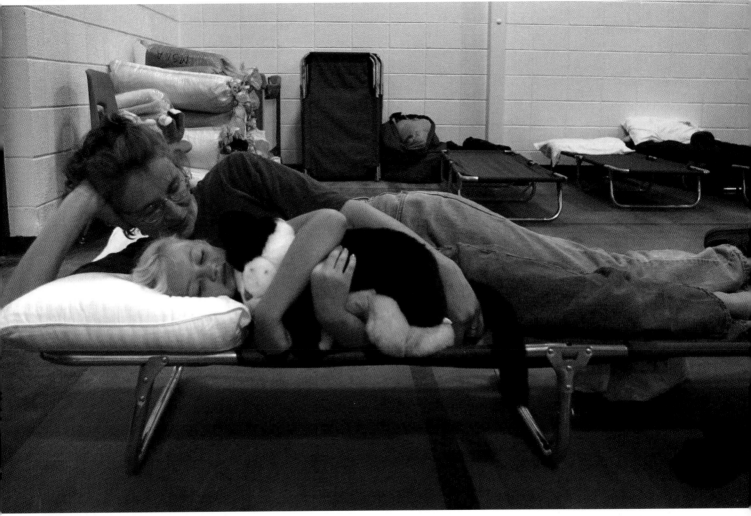

BLODGETT TRAILHEAD *Stacy Jessop and her eight-year-old daughter, Kirtlin, take a brief rest at the emergency shelter in Westview Junior High, Hamilton, after evacuating their Pinesdale home with only a half hour to pack.*

Facing page: **WILDERNESS COMPLEX** *What was left of a mailbox—and a home—in the Bitterroot Valley's Laird Creek.*

BLODGETT TRAILHEAD
Joan Warner, an evacuated Pinesdale resident, hugs a Red Cross worker in thanks for their help, masks, and hot meals.

MISSOULA *Looking south over Higgins Avenue in downtown Missoula on August 3, the day a Stage 2 air alert had been declared.*

TOM BAUER/MISSOULIAN

BLODGETT TRAILHEAD *Smoke from the Blodgett fire near Hamilton rises out of the mountains behind the town.*

NINEMILE COMPLEX *Army pilot Scott Traynor, right, navigated for pilot William Johnston as their Black Hawk helicopter flew above the Ninemile Valley transporting firefighters and equipment in late August.*

Facing page: **KOOTENAI COMPLEX** *Some of the hottest fires in the Kootenai Complex sent flames toward Pinkham Creek drainage houses, southwest of Eureka.*

CLEAR CREEK/RESERVATION COMPLEX *Eddie T. Dale, right, and Ro Rock, firefighters from the Navajo Indian Reservation, listened to their crew leader outline mop-up plans for the Clear Creek fire near Perma.*

Facing page: **THOMPSON FLAT COMPLEX** *A crew member of the Del Rosa Hotshots lights a back fire on the Landowner fire to protect a home in forest.*

VALLEY COMPLEX *In the southern end of the Bitterroot Valley, a chimney and foundation are what little remain of a home on the North Fork of Rye Creek.*

TOM BAUER/*MISSOULIAN*

JOE WESTON/*RAVALLI REPUBLIC*

VALLEY COMPLEX

Firefighters from Idaho's Colville National Forest work on extinguishing hotspots behind a home on the West Fork of the Bitterroot, southwest of Darby.

VALLEY COMPLEX *In the Sleeping Child area of the Bitterroot Valley, firefighters assigned to protect a lone home await as the Valley Complex moves toward it.*

KURT WILSON / *MISSOULIAN*

DARBY *Connie Holmquist, left, and Terri Blomberg comfort one another during the service at First Baptist Church in Darby on the Sunday after Blomberg's home was destroyed.*

Left: ***BLODGETT TRAILHEAD*** *Flames crest a ridge of the Bitterroot Mountains on the Blodgett fire near Pinesdale.*

Following pages: ***RYAN GULCH*** *Fire runs through the trees on the Ryan Gulch fire near Missoula.*

ALDER CREEK FIRE
A Sikorsky Sky Crane drops its load on the Alder Creek fire in the Rock Creek drainage.

MISSOULA *Staffers in the fire information center in Missoula look at fire maps to answer callers' questions.*

Right: **VALLEY COMPLEX** *Deer Mountain Fire Lookout survived in a charred area, and it soon was back in service.*

KURT WILSON /*MISSOULIAN*

BLODGETT TRAILHEAD A water-carrying helicopter heads toward the Blodgett fire near Pinesdale north of Hamilton.

DARBY Bill Zoebisch bows his head during a Sunday service
at First Baptist Church, Darby, in the midst of the fires.

VALLEY COMPLEX
Inspecting a burned area for leftover "smokes," or smoldering matter, is part of the mop-up process.

KURT WILSON /MISSOULIAN

WILDERNESS COMPLEX This deer was burned by the Little Blue fire near Painted Rocks Lake in the Bitterroot. Most healthy animals are able to escape wildfires.

KURT WILSON /MISSOULIAN

RYAN GULCH Soon after this truck traveled Interstate 90 past part of the Ryan Gulch fire near Beavertail Hill, the highway was closed.

Facing page: **BLODGETT TRAILHEAD** On the Blodgett Creek fire, a helicopter pilot dumps his water bucket, trying to keep flames from dropping down to accumulated duff on the Bitterroot Valley floor.

MICHAEL GALLACHER/*MISSOULIAN*

Right: **NINEMILE COMPLEX** *Plastic sheeting was in demand at the Ninemile fire camp on the first day of September, when much-needed rain turned the dusty tent town into a bog of wonderful mud.*

Below: **IDAHO** *Marines from Camp Pendleton, California react to a USO dance troupe in Salmon, Idaho. The troupe entertained Marines who were helping battle nearby forest fires.*

Facing page: **SKALKAHO COMPLEX** *The fire burned past the Skalkaho Highway home of Steve Baker, protected by an onsite fire crew, and sprinklers that Baker left running when he evacuated in the middle of the night.*

KURT WILSON /*MISSOULIAN*

KURT WILSON /MISSOULIAN

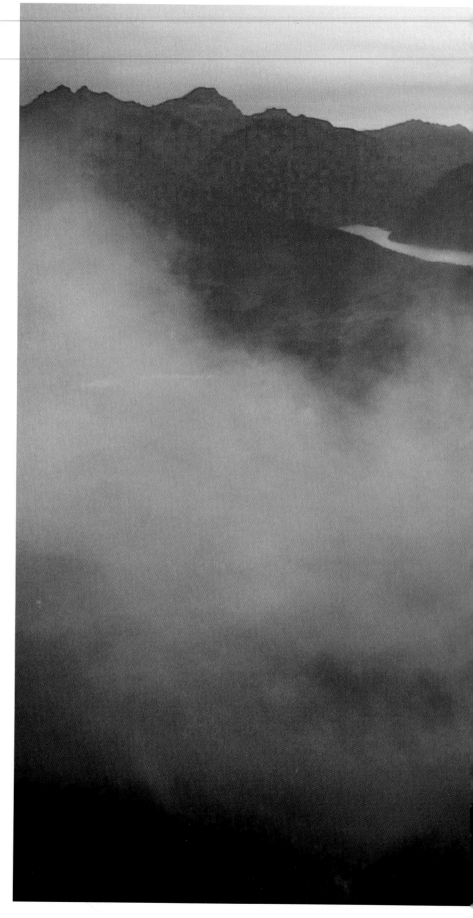

VALLEY COMPLEX *At sunset, an aerial view of the Valley Complex with Lake Como and the Bitterroot Range beyond.*

SULA COMPLEX *"The good Lord brought me here fifty-six years ago yesterday to be a good steward," said Margie Mikesell, a Bitterroot Valley rancher who, along with her husband John, ranches on the same land her parents did. "I didn't expect this." About thirty of the Mikesells' cows took off into the forest after Sula Complex flames opened their fence.*

Below: **BLODGETT TRAILHEAD** *An aerial tanker drops its load of fire retardant between the Blodgett fire and a home in the Bitterroot.*

SULA COMPLEX *John Snyder lifts a scorched wheelbarrow from the ashes of the summer home near Sula that he and wife Alberta had owned for three decades.*

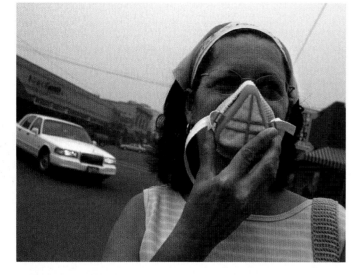

HAMILTON Jane Alvarez of Stevensville thought that shopping in downtown Hamilton in mid-August called for a breathing filter.

Right: **BLODGETT TRAILHEAD** Helicopters drop water on the Blodgett fire near Hamilton.

FRENCHTOWN When the offer was made for firefighters on the Ninemile blaze to attend Frenchtown's first high school football game of the season, about 300 soldiers from Fort Hood, Texas, accepted. Even better, rain poured down right after the game's kickoff.

Facing page: **MISSOULA** A slurry bomber drops a load of retardant on the leading edge of a grass fire on Missoula's north hills.

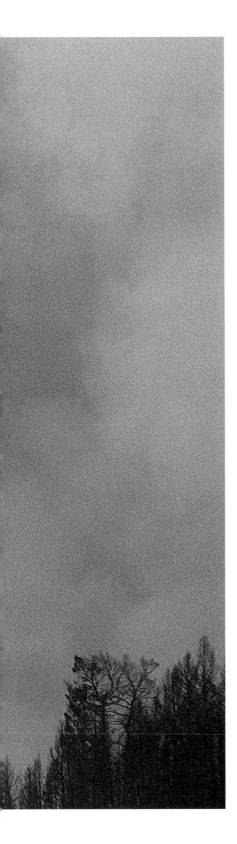

MAUDLOW-TOSTON COMPLEX Montana
National guardsmen work on putting out the
remains of a burning tree, on a hillside in
Deep Creek Canyon.

Left: **MAUDLOW-TOSTON COMPLEX**
Only three hours after its birth, the lusty infant
moved across ranchland northwest of Bozeman.

MAUDLOW-TOSTON COMPLEX *National Guardsmen scramble on a hillside to put out a hotspot.*

Above and below: **MAUDLOW-TOSTON COMPLEX** *Fire crews and the fire's nucleus on the ranch where a harvesting operation started the Maudlow-Toston fire.*

MAUDLOW-TOSTON COMPLEX *Near Dry Creek Road
and Ridge Road Junction.*

MAUDLOW-TOSTON COMPLEX *High temperatures and the high Montana elevation took a toll on Florida firefighter Pam McKitrick, second from right, who needed to pause while hiking up steep terrain near Meyers Gulch.*

MAUDLOW-TOSTON COMPLEX *Chuck Hahn (center) talked with neighbors Rici (left) and Don Collins on Ross Gulch Road after getting his cattle out of harm's way. Several ranchers scrambled to get their livestock to safety when the winds pushed the fire into Deep Creek Canyon.*

MAUDLOW-TOSTON COMPLEX *Montana National Army Guardsmen cheer a Blackhawk helicopter about to make a drop on a hotspot near them.*

MAUDLOW-TOSTON COMPLEX *A fireball blazes right by Highway 12 through Deep Creek Canyon.*

CANYON FERRY COMPLEX

Firefighters keep a watchful eye on the Bucksnort Fire while diverting it from nearby structures and burning out excess fuel inside the thick trees.

CANYON FERRY COMPLEX *A cabin off Magpie Creek Road after the Cave Gulch fire.*

Facing page: **CANYON FERRY COMPLEX** *The Cave Gulch Fire swept through the Grouse Creek area.*

CANYON FERRY COMPLEX
Local volunteer fire departments were the fire responders on Canyon Ferry Road along the Missouri River.

CANYON FERRY COMPLEX *The Bucksnort fire never crossed Canyon Ferry Reservoir's east-side road, leaving shoreline cabins and campgrounds untouched.*

JON EBELT/*INDEPENDENT RECORD*

CANYON FERRY COMPLEX The Bucksnort Fire swept through an area just off West Shore Drive near the Orchard Recreation Area, taking out a couple of vehicles and an apparent boat trailer.

CANYON FERRY COMPLEX

Firefighters Scott Perry (left) and Treavor Berg, of the Rae Fire Department near Bozeman, foam down trees to protect a nearby cabin.

CANYON FERRY COMPLEX

Flammables, like this pile of wooden beams, were left to burn as long as they threatened no structures.

CANYON FERRY COMPLEX *Tim Thaery (far left), Joe Kitowski, and Jay Kommers of the Rae Volunteer Fire Department take a few moments to catch their breath. They, along with crews from Manhattan and Amsterdam, were checking cabins on the west shore of Canyon Ferry Reservoir.*

CANYON FERRY COMPLEX *Ann Tanke gets her first look at her home after it was saved by retardant laid down by a slurry bomber.*

CANYON FERRY COMPLEX *Jennifer Ray, with son Travis, stopped during the evacuation of the Prickley Pear Valley north of East Helena in July to try to reach her husband.*

CANYON FERRY COMPLEX *Four hundred evacuees are addressed at an information meeting by Chris Hoff, incident commander.*

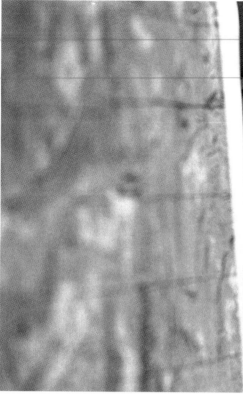

CANYON FERRY COMPLEX *Helena National forest Supervisor Tom Clifford waited for his turn to speak to the evacuees.*

CANYON FERRY COMPLEX *The brick floor of what was a cabin on the west shore of Canyon Ferry Reservoir glowed from intense heat that had burned it to the ground.*

CANYON FERRY COMPLEX *Smoke billowed from the Cave Bay fire as morning winds whipped the fire back into an inferno, with flames reaching as high as 100 feet.*

BOULDER COMPLEX
The Ontario 13 Crew arrives at the High Ore fire.

Right: **CANYON FERRY COMPLEX**
Montana Highway Patrol officer Joe Cohenour motions to a motorist to turn around after Spokane Hills Road was closed.

Facing page: **CANYON FERRY COMPLEX**
Firefighter Gary Markley of Sultan, Washington, is surrounded by steam while hosing down a burned area in the Spokane Hills.

CANYON FERRY COMPLEX *Flames rise high into the night sky along the top of the Spokane Hills, on the west shore of Canyon Ferry Reservoir, a few miles east of Helena.*

GEORGE LANE/*INDEPENDENT RECORD*

HELENA *Smoke from the Toston-Maudlow fire created beautiful sunrises, but also caused health concerns.*

CANYON FERRY COMPLEX *Near miss for a West Shore Drive home at Canyon Ferry Reservoir.*

BOULDER COMPLEX *Smoke billows into the sky as winds whip the fire on Interstate 15's Boulder Hill.*

CANYON FERRY COMPLEX *The fire above Magpie Bay.*

BOULDER COMPLEX *The Ontario 13 Crew and a Sikorsky Sky Crane*
battle a flare-up on the High Ore fire.

BOULDER COMPLEX
Carl Grant, of the Blackfeet #42 Firecrew, is decked out in colorful bandannas to handle the smoke and the sweat that are part of firefighting.

BOULDER COMPLEX Two Forest Service firefighters reviewing a tree that blazed in a flare-up on the High Ore fire. In the background, the Ontario 13 Crew digs a line to contain the fire. The white on the ground is retardant foam.

BOULDER COMPLEX *A BPA linemen walks out on one of the dead 500,000-volt powerlines in preparation to hoist a inspection basket.*

CRAIG M. MOORE

BOULDER COMPLEX
National Forest Service firefighter getting the daily news and shift plans from the base camp information board.

BOULDER COMPLEX *Sky Crane helicopter fills its 1500-gallon bucket to dump on up Muskrat Creek drainage.*

BOULDER COMPLEX *Boulder Hill fire,*
about to be fed by dry thunderstorms.

BOULDER COMPLEX *Jack Kendley of the Helena National Forest inspected Wickes after the High Ore fire tore through.*

CRAIG M. MOORE

BOULDER COMPLEX *Toys in Wickes after the fire.*

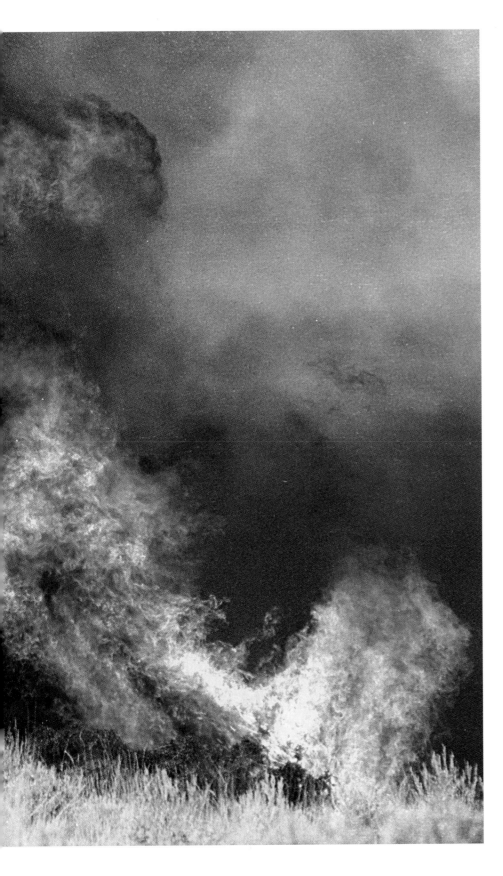

BILLINGS *A volunteer fire-fighter battles a range fire along Duck Creek near Billings in mid-August.*

WILLIE FIRE With a backdrop of thick smoke, singer Willie Nelson entertained an enthusiastic crowd at the Red Lodge rodeo grounds at the end of August. The blaze was dubbed the Willie Fire in honor of the entertainer.

WILLIE FIRE The motorcycle that caused the Willie fire crashed six miles south of Red Lodge on the Beartooth Highway.

BILLINGS *Volunteer firefighters man a water pump along a roadway hoping to stop a fire's spread east of Billings.*

LARRY MAYER/*BILLINGS GAZETTE*

WILLIE FIRE *Smoke billows over Red Lodge in this aerial view of the wildfire that forced evacuations on Rock Creek.*

Right: **BILLINGS**
C.J. and Tucker Marquart wait in Billings for their father, Arnie Marquart, an Army National Guardsman, to return from fighting fires.

Below: **WILLIE FIRE**
Highway 212, the scenic Beartooth Highway, was closed at the height of tourist season.

LARRY MAYER/*BILLINGS GAZETTE*

KEN BLACKBIRD/*BILLINGS GAZETTE*

EPILOGUE

Excerpts from Governor Marc Racicot's remarks at a Hamilton town meeting, September 5, 2000

KURT WILSON/*MISSOULIAN*

Governor Marc Racicot thanks firefighters from the California Department of Forestry and Fire Protection before they board a plane for home.

There's probably not very much that I could tell you about disasters that you don't already know, having lived in the eye of the hurricane for some period of time now. And of course you've received all of the technical briefings from a perspective of all of those who have been engaged in heroic fashion in battling these blazes.

When I stand up to talk to you about these particular issues of course I, like you, am moved and inspired by the extraordinary dedication of so many people, so many friends and neighbors, people who work for volunteer fire departments, those who live next door to one another, soldiers from all over the country and from all over the continent, people from thirty-nine different states, people that have been coming here from foreign countries, all standing shoulder to shoulder and addressing all of these issues that have confronted us here in the state of Montana. And you simply can't help but be inspired by such an exceptional dedication as all of these people have demonstrated.

This has been the largest mobilization of personnel, resources, technology and machinery to a single disaster in the history of the United States of America. We know that something extraordinarily difficult and catastrophic has happened here in our state by that measure alone.

But for every Montanan or everyone who loves Montana, and I suspect that is a vast majority of people in the United States of America, there is something sad that has happened here as well, and something that has been gripping and difficult emotionally to deal with. That covers the entire age spectrum, from those who are older (as I am becoming), and those who are younger, who have sensed the cares and concerns emanating from their parents and from their grandparents and from members of their families, and of course through their own perceptions, seeing the smoke and hearing sirens and the planes flying overhead and knowing that something very unusual was happening here in the state of Montana.

So, we have been through some trying times and we have marshaled together virtually every asset and resource we know how to bring to bear to focus upon these issues. And we have called upon friends and neighbors all over the planet and they have responded, and universally they have been overwhelmed with the character of the people of the state of Montana and with their demonstration of kindness and tolerance and, perhaps most importantly, their ability to endure.

Not many people quote Calvin Coolidge any more. In fact, I'm not altogether certain how many people ever quoted Calvin Coolidge. But he did say something that appears to me to be strikingly important to remember tonight. And that is: all that really matters is endurance. ...Calvin Coolidge said that the world was full of unfulfilled genius. He said ultimately those who endured were the ones who ultimately succeeded. And that, I think, is a quality of character that Montanans share in large measure, uniquely, on this planet. We will endure and we will persist in our efforts, and we will succeed....

We may not always agree. I have noticed that, in my service to you, we are inclined to share candid thoughts with one another, which I think provides an opportunity for us to grow. But, in the end, we will come together and we will address these issues and we will become what all of us want to be as a state, and we will make certain that we live up to the expectations of one another.

I know, as we address the fire's damage, we can take comfort and thank God for sparing each human life associated with fighting it. We have expended many resources, lost treasures that we relied on, but, thankfully, no one we love.

The damages— they are extraordinary. We have been, in the state of Montana, going through an exceptionally large amount of resources, as you might imagine. We've probably spent close to $200 million in the state of Montana alone. And firefighting costs across the western United States will approach a billion dollars...And that's just the suppression costs alone. We don't know precisely, yet, how much Montana will be responsible for. But we have received some unprecedented assistance from the federal government.

First of all, we've had partnerships with the Forest Service, with the BLM and FEMA and the Small Business Administration that I believe each of you would be proud of and find to be inspiring. People have worked together without concern for any parochial interests and have dedicated themselves exclusively, as a team, to addressing all of the fire issues. And that includes not only the federal agencies, but the state and local agencies all working together, as well.

So we have a lot of work to do. A lot of work has been done, but we have a lot of work left to be done to address all of the issues that not only have to do with suppression but also with the recovery, rehabilitation and reclamation efforts...So we're going to be working very hard...

I wish somehow there was something, some way that we could communicate...how grateful all those who have visited here and worked here feel for the kindnesses that have been extended to them, which seems to me to be ironic in some respects. Yet somehow, because of the conduct and demeanor of Montanans, they feel this strange sense of gratitude at being invited here to fight fire, to breathe smoke, to get dirty and grimy and possibly to be subjected to all kinds of different threats, including even the possibility of losing their lives. They say they are grateful for having had the opportunity.

It says to me something awfully special about the people of the state of Montana. I know that I am certainly proud and grateful for the opportunity to serve you and to work with you through this process. But I hope you, too, feel a collective and an individual sense of pride in how Montana has revealed itself, through its people, to the rest of the world.

PEASE FIRE *On the Crow Indian Reservation, this fire quickly affected 4,612 acres and destroyed one full-time residence at the end of August.*

ABOUT THE AUTHOR Michael Moore, 44, has spent the last 15 years as a reporter for the *Missoulian*. He's covered numerous fires, including the 1988 Canyon Creek blaze. In fact, his first big story for the paper was about a Forest Service worker who was tricked into setting a fire that eventually burned much of Missoula's Mount Sentinel and Hellgate Canyon in 1985. His stories have appeared in newspapers around the country, including the *New York Times*, the *San Francisco Examiner* and the *Los Angeles Times*, as well as several magazines.

In his non-professional life, Moore is a fisherman, a guitarist, a hunter and a whitewater rafter. He has a 15-year-old daughter, who is his constant snowboarding companion.